Charles Barton Bovill (1911 - 2001), a Bedford School boy in the late-1910s and early-1920s, played a key role during World War Two in the creation and deployment of Eureka and the S-phone, radio equipment that greatly improved ground-to-air communications between radio operators in RAF planes and secret agents and Resistance groups on the ground. After the war he was involved in Electronic Counter Surveillance, designing sophisticated equipment for the Intelligence services, the Security services and private companies. So well respected were some of Charles's devices that they were used in James Bond films.

Charles was born on February 18th, 1911 at Battersea, south London, the second son of Ethel and Charles H. Bovill. His father was a successful playwright who wrote the lyrics for five musicals and employed a youthful P. G. Wodehouse (1881 – 1975), the successful English comic novelist, as an assistant. Wodehouse was famous for his humorous accounts of life in upper-class English society featuring Bertie Wooster, the eccentric aristocrat and Jeeves, his butler. They had several short stories published in the *Strand* in London and in the *Pictorial Review* in the United States and a number of plays running in theatres in the West End of London .

Charles was brought up at The Knowle, a 17th century cottage in Barcombe, a small rural village in Sussex between Brighton and Eastbourne, and attended Revd. E. Griffith's Grammar School in Lewes.

Following the outbreak of the First World War in 1914 Charles' father served as a Lieutenant but, like millions of others, was killed fighting on the Western Front.

Ethel, his mother, took the boys to Bedford and found accommodation at 32 Clapham Road. Whether she already had connections in the town is unknown. Edward, Charles' nine-year old brother, started at Bedford Preparatory School in September 1918 and he started the following year when he was seven. Charles' school record shows he was put in the 4th Division of Year One. Numerous absences were noted, attributed presumably to a note that he had a "weak heart." In fact, he was abroad for the whole of 1923.

According to his obituary in *The Daily Telegraph*, Charles was sent to the Mediterranean coast of France to be brought up by his aunt, a formidable character who, it was said, was well known to Wodehouse. Several of his aunt's traits were included in Wodehouse's fearsome character, Aunt Agatha, who "eats broken bottles, wears barbed wire next to the skin and offers human sacrifices at the time of the full moon."

Whether his experiences with this "nephew crusher" convinced him that he had to return to school is unknown, but his records show that he restarted in 1924. He joined the Mathematical group, as opposed to the Classical, and progressed to the 2nd Division before leaving at Easter 1925 when he was only fourteen.

The 1920s saw a craze in making what were called 'crystal sets'. These were do-it-yourself radio kits, as pre-assembled models were not then available. Charles's Science teachers at Bedford School probably encouraged him to read the popular Science magazines that could be found in the library or bought in shops in the town. In many of them he would have found instructions of building a crystal set. Maybe he made one in lessons?

Boy Scouts, very popular in the 1920s, had lessons in making them. Should he or his teachers have smoked they could have found instructions on printed cards found inside every pack of Philip Godfrey cigarette packets. These sets used an antenna wire wrapped around a Quaker Oats or other cereal packet, and were tuned by touching a 'cat's whisker' or diode to a mineral crystal. The radio waves could then be listened to using early headphones.

Edward was more academic at school. He left Bedford the following year when he was seventeen and followed his father's military footsteps, being accepted at the Royal Military Academy at Sandhurst, in Surrey with a Prize Cadetship. In 1928 he joined the Royal Tank regiment but died four years later of typhoid fever in Peshawar, close to what is now the Indian/Pakistan border in the Punjab.

Where Charles went after leaving school is unknown, possibly back to France, as he went on to study radio at the University of Grenoble and then at Regent Street Polytechnic in central London. When he graduated he did not get a job working with radio straight away. He found employment in the meat trade in the Smithfield area of the city. But it was not his choice of career. As a young man in the 'swinging twenties' he needed money. In an interview he gave in 1994 to Klas Nilsson, the Chief Executive Officer of Security Manager, Sweden, he shed light on what happened after he left.

We were pretty poor when I started this business. I used to carry meat around from this meat market, and I didn't like it. And I used to go home every weekend to a place called Bedford, to see my mother and to keep an eye on her. One day I met a man much older than I was, who asked me what my job was. So I told him that I wanted to get into electrical engineering and had studied radio at the University of Grenoble in France. This was a very long time ago, 1928. He said, "Forget the meat market. I will give you a job. Get a few books about electricity and start with me next month." I had two enjoyable years with him. I will not go into the reasons I left. But in 1933 I was not working and went down to the motor racing course at Brooklands [near Weybridge, Surrey] where I met an old school friend and told him of my hope of getting into radio. To my surprise he said go and see my brother at His Masters Voice. (HMV had a factory in Hayes, Middlesex.) I went and was very happy there developing domestic radios. Learned everything I wanted to. I went to night schools two or three times a week. The war was by then in the offing and I was offered a job by the Air Ministry as a inspector of RAF radio equipment. (The Royal Air Force had their headquarters at Adastral House on Kingsway, London.) *I was awfully bored and they did not like me and I did not like them. I must be able to do something. I didn't like to waste my talents. I applied for a job in the Air Division of Marconi's and got it. The date was January 3rd 1938 and was one of the great days of my life. Everything went perfectly for me.*

(http://securityriskmanagement.eu/content1.asp?
cID=charlesbovill-en 12th December 2009)

The Marconi Wireless Telegraph Company had a radio factory in Chelmsford, Essex. Whilst there he probably met Christopher Cockerell, a senior engineer with Marconi from 1935 to 1951, who was later given a knighthood for his invention of the Hovercraft. Charles' work involved working with the radio equipment that Marconi sold to civilian aircraft companies.

As war approached, Marconi arranged for Charles to go and work with RAF Bomber and Coastal Command as a wireless development engineer where he had to liaise between them and the company. He was aware that the existing radio equipment on the RAF's planes was of a very old design. After the first bombing raid of Germany in May 1940, it became apparent to Charles that the RAF needed more up-to-date radio equipment.

Marconi was asked to carry out trials with all RAF bomber types using the company's latest model which was already fitted to many of the country's civilian aircraft. Charles carried out all the tests on what he called AD77. According to the Duxford Radio

Society, this was one of Marconi's existing transmitters. Following these checks, he supervised the fitting of hundreds of Hampden, Blenhiem, Whitely and Wellington bombers and made many test flights in them. By 1945 Marconi had made about 30,000 of these sets for Bomber Command.

Following the German invasion of France and the Low Countries on 15th May 1940, Marshal Petain, the French military leader, signed the Armistice. In the summer of 1940, the Secret Intelligence Service (SIS), the covert section of the Foreign Office, approached the Air Ministry with the suggestion that they experiment into how feasible it would be to parachute agents and land aircraft into enemy territory to pick up and bring back VIPs (Very Important Persons). They recognized that they would be very useful with the Allies' war effort. Many military and diplomatic personnel had been left behind after the evacuation from Dunkirk at the end of May. Some merged into the local population and helped train them clandestinely to oppose the German assimilation of the conquered territories. It was essential that some of these people needed bringing back to England occasionally for additional training and then sent back with funds to support the various resistance groups.

The urgency of the situation was taken on board and Winston Churchill, the British Prime Minister, set up the Special Operations Executive (SOE) with a directive *"to set Europe ablaze."* Their operations were to be 'unattributable' industrial sabotage, the raising and supplying of secret armies and collecting intelligence information, all done under what Michael Foot, the SOE historian, described as *"the dense fog of secrecy."* Those 'in the know' called it the Inter-Services Research Bureau (ISRB). Its five-floor office block at 64 Baker Street in London was just down the road from the flat occupied by Sherlock Holmes, Sir Arthur Conan Doyle's fictitious detective,

Given the nature of its work, the SOE Headquarters had to have War Department cover so the name MOI (SP) was coined and its telephone number added to the War Office's directory. Captain

Peter Lee, an officer in its security section, was quoted as saying that *"it was terribly clever. We said it stood for 'Mysterious Operations in Special Places'. We reckoned the Germans, with their lack of sense of humour, would never be able to unravel that one."*

London gradually introduced clandestine operations into occupied Europe in an attempt to destabilise the German forces. Under the cover of night, some secret agents were taken by boat or submarine and dropped on isolated French beaches. Important military, political and commercial personnel were returned safely to south coast ports but, as the Atlantic Wall, an extensive network of coastal fortifications stretching from Norway to Spain, was completed, this method became increasingly dangerous.

1419 Special Duties Squadron, operating from Newmarket racecourse in Cambridgeshire, flew out on the few nights available between the waxing and waning of the moon to drop agents and supplies into occupied Europe. Pilots had to fly low, often below 100 feet (37m) above sea level, to avoid enemy radar. They did not use lights so they could avoid the attention of the people manning the searchlights and flak batteries. (The word flak comes from the German Fliegerabwehrkanone, aircraft defence cannon.) As they were not on bombing missions they had to avoid built-up areas and Luftwaffe controlled airfields where night fighter planes were based.

The only available maps of France that the RAF navigators could study were first-edition ones that had not been updated since the 19th century. Aerial recognition of the landscape had to have the assistance of the moon. Its reflection from ponds, lakes, streams, rivers, canals and railway lines helped orientate the pilots. In remote areas they recognised that the darkest areas were forest and the lighter areas fields. Occasionally, car headlights from a doctor on an emergency mission provided useful illumination as the Germans had introduced the blackout and night curfews.

Pinpointing what was called the 'drop zone' or DZ demanded excellent navigation skills but Charles and his fellow 'boffins', the term used to describe scientific experts, came to their aid. Following the Air Ministry's substantial success developing and employing defensive radar during the Battle of Britain in 1940, the boffins at Telecommunications Research Establishment (TRE) based at Worth Maltravers, near Swanage in Dorset, came up with some new ideas. A small ground-based radar beacon was developed which could emit a signal which could be picked up by receiving equipment on board an airplane. It allowed its operator to determine both the location and the distance of ships and planes. The word 'Radar', an acronym for radio detection and ranging, remained restricted until June 1943, when the Allies released the term to the public.

This top-secret technology was to dramatically improve clandestine night-time air navigation. It was in Beryl Escott's *Mission Improbable* that she mentions John I. Brown as the designer and world expert of a team which, in the age before transistors, managed to produce a succession of radio equipment for SOE, each an improvement on, and smaller than, the last.

TRE personnel nicknamed the ground portion of this equipment 'Eureka', and the airborne counterpart 'Rebecca'. They began developing test sets for the RAF's Special Duties Squadrons who were flying out on top secret missions. Eureka to become an invaluable piece of portable electronic equipment carried by agents of the SIS, SOE, the Special Armed Services (SAS) and the American Office of Strategic Services (OSS). It was a compact radar navigation homing beacon named after the Greek expression, "I have found it." Science students will recall that "Eureka' was shouted out by Archimedes when he understood what happened when he got into the bath. Rebecca is said to have been named after a character in the Old Testament, the wife of Isaac, who was described as crying out for her twins, Esau and Jacob.

Charles's work in Bomber and Coastal Command brought him to the attention of the Special Operations

Executive (SOE) and, in October 1941, he was invited to command the radio experimental and flight section of the ISRB. They were very keen on him developing a new radio telephone system.

In the autumn of 1941 I was summoned to an office in Baker St. London where I was interviewed by an Army officer who spoke to me in French. I remarked to him that he had a French Canadian accent and from that moment we got on very well and I was offered the job if I could join them in a month. I was able to arrange this with Marconi's and found myself as a civilian developing the S-phone for the Special Operations Executive (SOE). This work, its development and operations is described in an article which I wrote for the British technical journal the 'Electronic world + Wireless World' in September 1993.

Briefly, the S-phone was a duplex UHF radio for use by the resistance for contacting aircraft on parachute drops and for the passing of intelligence to high-flying aircraft. It only had a range of less than a kilometre ground to ground, Thousands of operations took place but it was never detected by the Germans. Flying at 25,000 feet, contact was possible at 50 miles (80km). Soon after joining SOE I was commissioned in the RAF and worked with the Special Duties Squadrons - 138 and 161, which did all of the dropping of supplies to the resistance groups in Europe

(Ibid.)

The 'Ground' transceiver was designed by Captain Bert Lane, and the 'Air' transceiver by Major Hobday, both of the Royal Signals Corps. The S-phone's principal asset was its ability to reduce agents' dread of detection. As it was designed to be able to be carried in a suitcase, the phone enabled SOE-designated aircrew and agents in the field to talk to each other with very little risk of interception. It was also used effectively between motor gunboats landing agents and reception parties on French Mediterranean beaches. In adverse weather conditions like mist, fog and low

Charles Bovill (1911—2001)

The Knowle, Barcombe, Sussex, a 17th century cottage where
Charles Bovill spent part of his early childhood.

http://www.bandhpast.co.uk/barcombe/b0428build.php11th Januray 2010)

Front covers of one of Charles' father's collaborations
with P. G. Wodehouse

32 Clapham Road, Bedford, where Ethel Bovill lived whilst her
sons, Edward and Charles, attended Bedford School 1918—1925

(Photographed by author, 13th Jan 2010)

Charles Bovill (1911—2001)

Charles' elder brother and fellow Old Bedfordian, 2nd
Lieutenant Edward Henry Bovill, died in Peshawar in
1935, aged 28.
www.gommecourt.co.uk/.../QWR/Bovill%20QWR1.jpg 11th January 2010

Charles Bovill (1911–2001)

Listening to a radio set in the 1920s was a new experience. Boys
were keen followers of this new technology.

(1920s.www.wired.com/.../2008/09/radio_1921_630px.jpg 10th January 2010)

So were girls. An early-1920s radio set with a 'scientific appearance'
from an original painting by Jenny Nystrom.
(http://www.historyofpa.co.uk/gfx/cw/2lo/girl.jpg 4th February 2010)

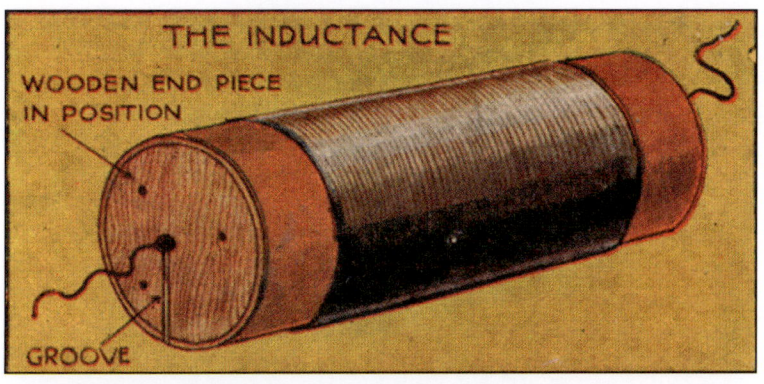

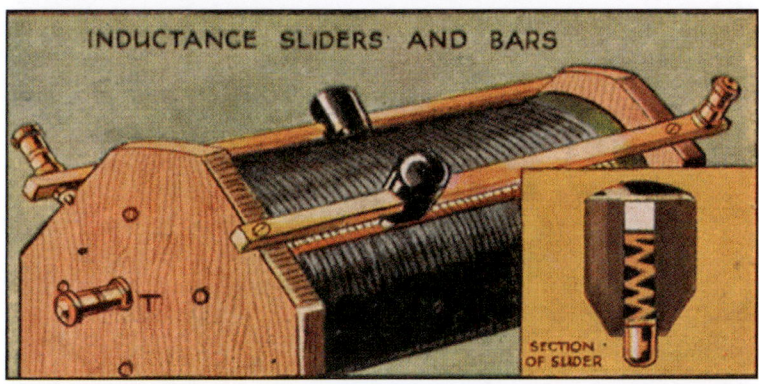

Cards issued with Godfrey Phillips Cigarettes in the early to mid-1920s.
(www.r-type.org/static/crystal.htm 10th January 2010)

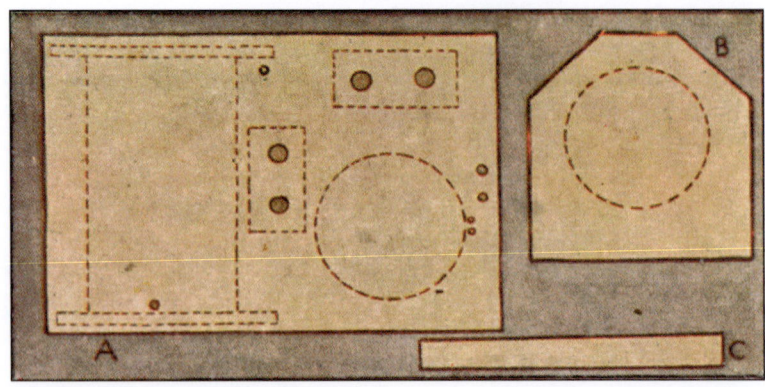

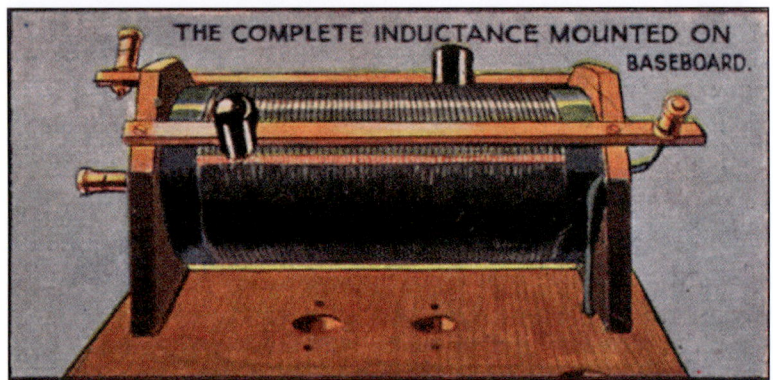

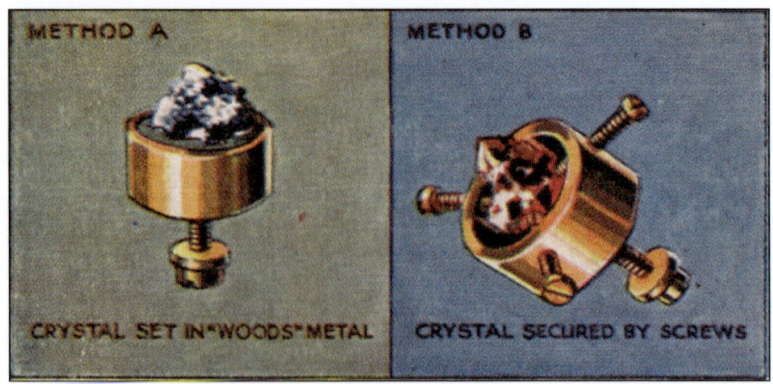

Cards issued with Godfrey Phillips Cigarettes in the early to mid-1920s.
(www.r-type.org/static/crystal.htm 10th January 2010)

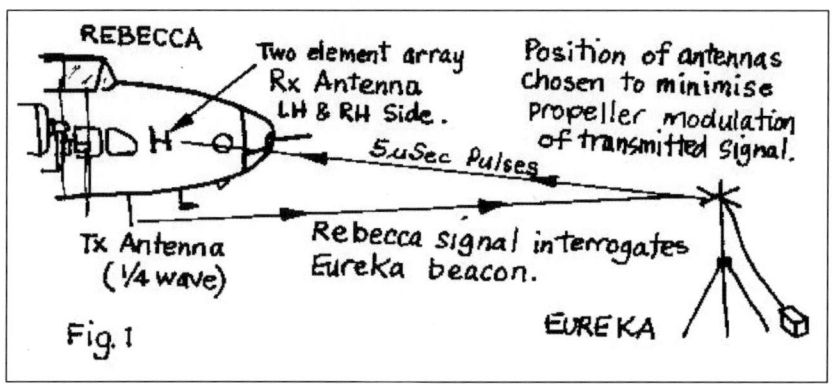

(http://www.duxfordradiosociety.org/equiphist/reb-eureka/eureka-fig1-598p.jpg 14th December 2009)

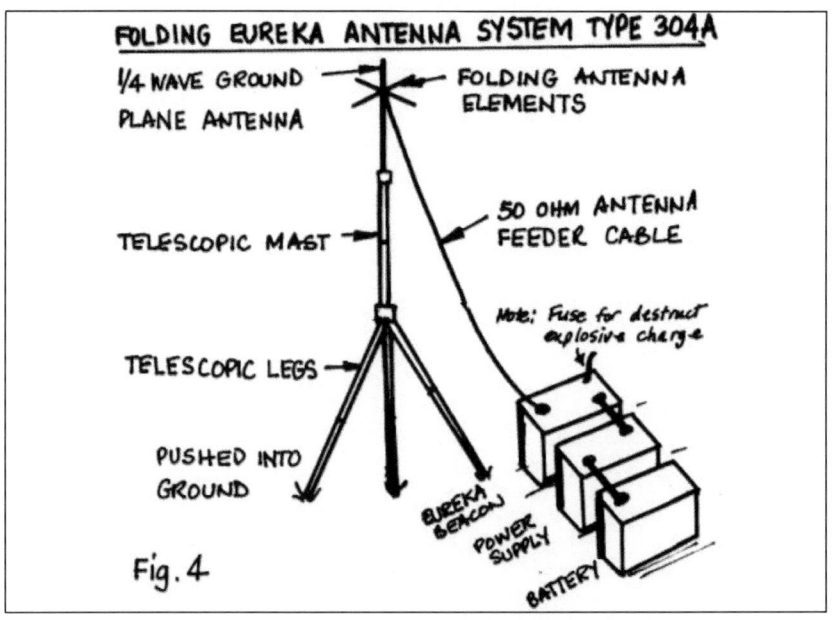

(http://www.duxfordradiosociety.org/equiphist/reb-eureka/eureka-fig4-640p.jpg 14th December 2009)

Charles Bovill (1911—2001)

Eureka Unit

(http://histru.bournemouth.ac.uk/Oral_History/Talking_About_Technology/radar_research/assets/
images/p57-img2.gif 14th December 2009)

Rebecca Unit

(http://www.duxfordradiosociety.org/equiphist/reb-eureka/ind96-100-1.jpg 14th December 2009)

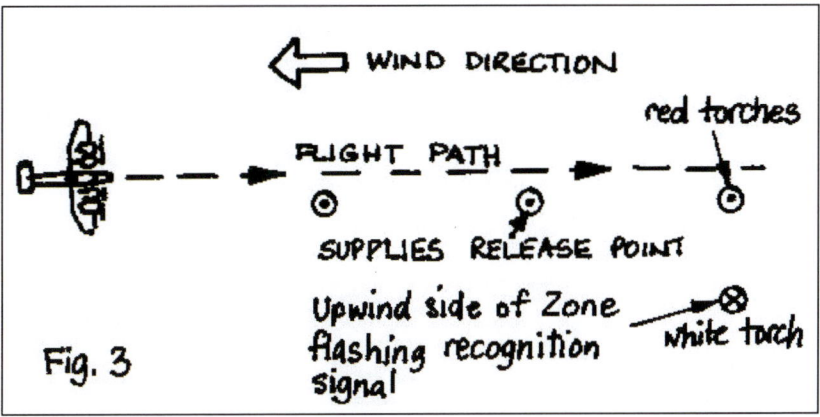

Fig. 3

The L-shaped layout of lights needed for a drop. The reception committee would place the Eureka unit nearby and light the torches when they heard the aircraft approaching. The S-Phone allowed vital messages to be sent to the radio operator on the plane who would then send them to SOE, SIS, SAS or OSS HQ when the plane returned to RAF Tempsford.

(http://www.duxfordradiosociety.org/equiphist/reb-eureka/eureka-fig3-601p.jpg 14th December 2009)

Training to use the S-Phone. Ten-day intensive courses were run for reception committee personnel at Howbury Hall, Renhold, Bedford, only five miles (8km) from RAF Tempsford..
(www.cvni.net/radio/e2k/e2k035/e2k35cs.html 19th December 2009)

Using the S-Phone in daylight. It was normally used at night.
http://www.pathfindergroupuk.com/2005/p_ruvien%20au%20S-Phone.jpg 14th December 2009

Gibraltar Farm, RAF Tempsford, Bedfordshire, nerve centre of operations on a n airfield designed by an illusionist to look disused. Hitler was said to be aware of this' viper's nest' but it was never attacked throughout the war.
(Courtesy of John Button)

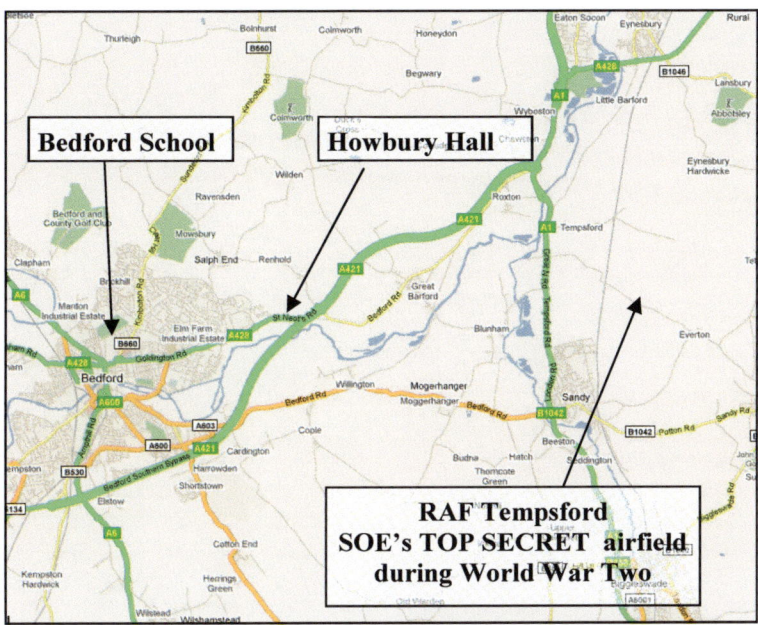

Google map extract showing places in Bedfordshire important in
Charles Bovill's life.

Photography of **Howbury Hall**, near Renhold, east of Bedford. During
World War Two it was requisitioned and agents were trained in
the latest Eureka and S-phone equipment before being flown out
of RAF Tempsford.
(Bernard O'Connor)

19

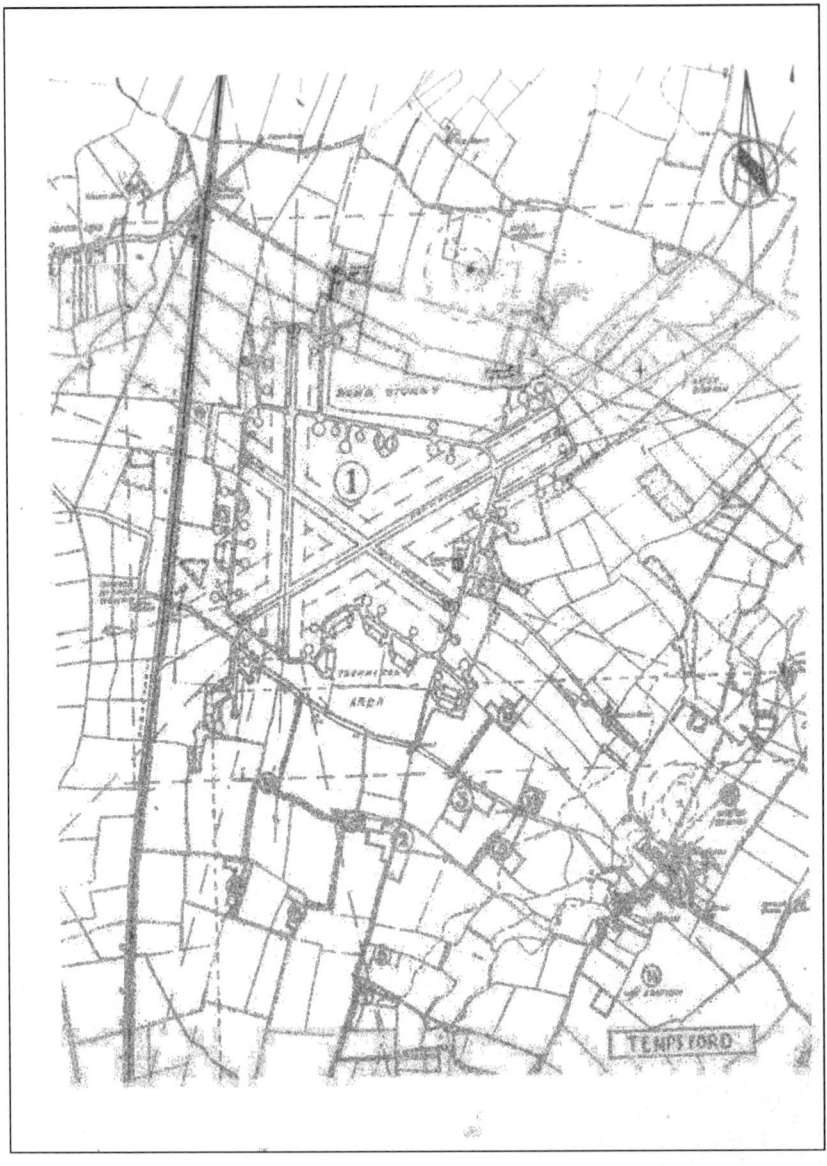

RAF Tempsford, Bedfordshire, home of 138 and 161 Special Duties
Squadrons during World War Two. Agents and supplies were flown out
from here on TOP SECRET missions to help resistance groups in
occupied Europe.
(Courtesy of RAF Hendon)

One of 138 Squadron's Stirling bombers modified to carry agents and supplies and equipped with Rebecca to allow radio communication with the reception committee.
(Courtesy of Bill Bright)

Westland Lysander used to take and pick up agents and VIPs from RAF Tempsford (and RAF Tangmere on south coast). Note the ladder to allow quicker access for the agents.
(www.jaapteeuwen.com/.../westland%20lysander.jpg 18th December 2009)

Lockheed Hudson used to land and pick up agents and VIPs in occupied Europe.
(www.2iemeguerre.com/avions/images/image1468.jpg 18th December 2009)

Modified Halifax Bomber used by Special Duties Squadrons (lost over
Czechoslovakia on 15th March 1943).
(www.harringtonmuseum.org.uk/138%20Halifax.jpg 18th December 2009)

Charles explaining some of his surveillance equipment
(Courtesy of Klas Nilsson)

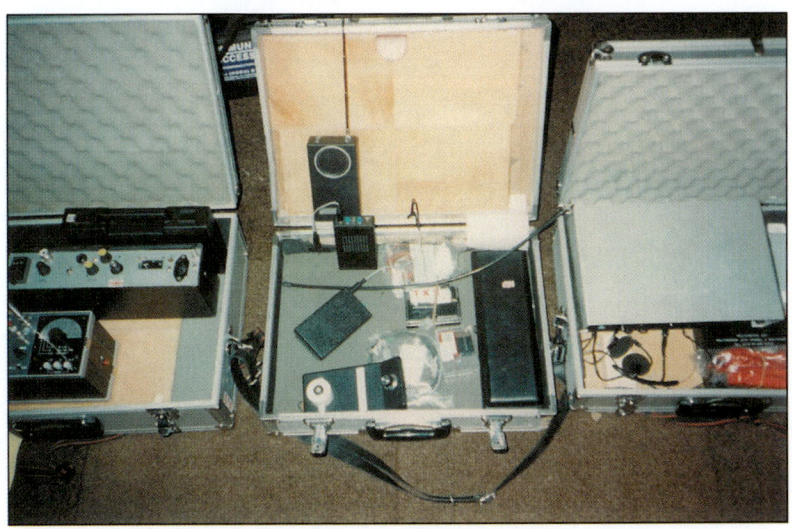

Electronic Counter Surveillance equipment taken by Charles Bovill to
demonstrate at conferences.
(Courtesy of Klas Nilsson)

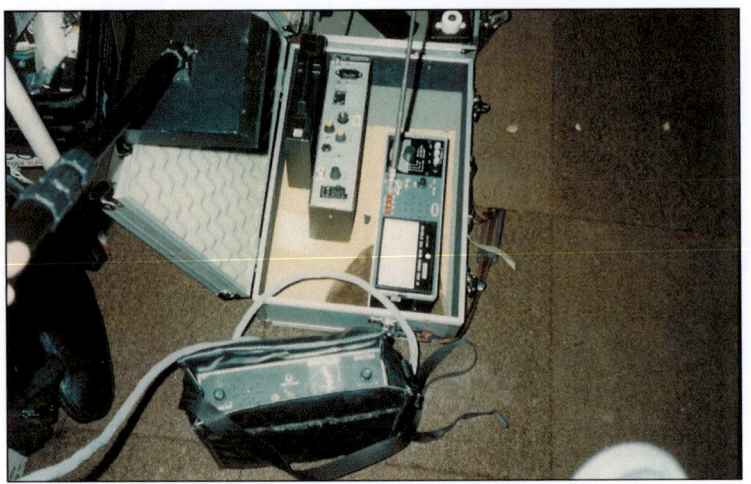

Charles's 'Broom' - electronic surveillance equipment
(Courtesy of Klas Nilsson)

ANTI-SURVEILLANCE ELECTRONIC EQUIPMENT

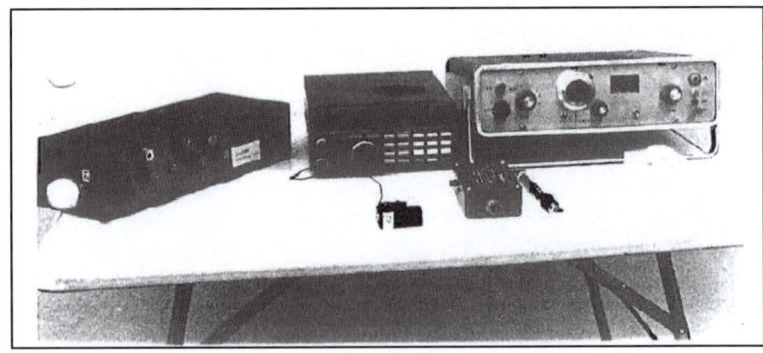

LOW FREQUENCY RECEIVER 10KHz TO 600 KHz FM, AM Sens: 2uV	TYPE 9600 RECEIVER 60 to 960 MHz FM,AM,SSB Subcarrier	BDRECEIVER 20 MHz to 1GHz FM, AM and Subcarrier BDRec Charger

Extract from an Electronic Surveillance Brochure
(Courtesy of Klas Nilsson)

CHARLES B BOVILL

C.Eng_, M.LE.E., F.I.E.R.E., M.R_Ae.S.

V AT No. 2129068 74

NON-LINEAR JUNCTION DETECTOR

The instrument consists of two basic items:

1. The detector unit which is slung over the shoulder when operating
2. The Search Antenna. This has a telescopic handle extending to five feet.
   It is used to sweep over the luggage being checked.

Indication of the presence of any item, whether switched on or off, is given by an audible like sound.

(Extract from an Electronic Surveillance Brochure courtesy of Klas Nilsson)

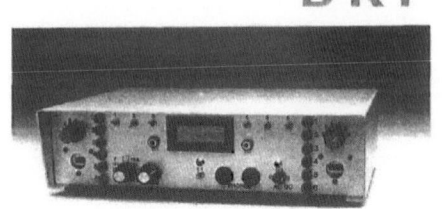

T

"B K I"

TELEPHONE
CHECKING
EQUIPMENT

BKI is an easy to use unit designed for the rapid testing of telephone instruments and lines. It is small in size and weighs only 6lbs.

The design is based upon the break-in method, and overcomes many of the problems in testing modern electronic communications.

BKI eliminates the need for making connections to any parts of the telephone system except between the new wall type sockets and the instrument.

A built-in digital volt-ammeter checks on-and-off hook conditions. There are outputs to a headset and tape recorder. Accessories are provided for connection to all known terminals.

A comprehensive switching system enables tests to be made for unauthorised attachments, line taps and phantom circuits.

The BKI has a rechargeable self-contained battery which will operate for 30 hours between charges.

When used in conjunction with Larsen, Broom and SR7, the BKI completes the range of equipment needed for total counter-surveillance operations.

The equipment can be used on 1 wire or 6 wire systems. The digital volt ammeter can be isolated from the internal circuits enabling it to be used as an independent instrument.

SENSITIVITY: For functions of volt ammeter a 50mV output to headset.

POWER CONSUMPTION (Battery operated) at full audio output 50mA

CHARGER: AC power consumption 10Q. Charger input voltage 115/210V (1060Hz) Fused

CONTROLS: On/Off with LED. 2 six position rotary switches, 6 toggle switches for cross line testing. 5 position meter switch: 0 20V. 0 200V, 0 20mA 0 200mA, AUDIOGAIN (Variable)

INPUTS/OUTPUTS: Socket for external use of volt ammeter. When used in this mode a switch solates the meter. 2 input sockets, 2 telephone jacks, Charger socket with Charging LED.

FINISH: Brushed aluminium case. Switches and input sockets colour coded.

DIMENSIONS: 300 x 76 x 211 mm, 12" x 3" x 8". Weight 2.7kg, 6lbs.

ACCESSORIES: Instructions, Set of adaptor cables, Headset, Attache carrying case.

SECURITY RESEARCH AND DEVELOPMENT LTD

cloud, a combination of Eureka and the S-phone could help to improve the RAF's accuracy when dropping weapons, supplies and people.

Reunited with one of the old phones for a TV documentary, Charles recalled how invaluable they were, "*A lot of people spoke so nicely about it... pilots I knew said it saved their lives, I felt that made everything worthwhile.*" (Channel 4 series, *The Spying Game, Are you receiving me?* Saturday 13th February, 1999)

1419 Special Duties Squadron was renamed 419 Squadron and finally 138 Squadron when it was transferred from Newmarket to a newly completed airfield at Tempsford, about eight miles (12km) east of Bedford on 1st March 1942. It had four Wellington Mark III bombers specially modified to trial TR 1335 or 'GEE', another radio navigation system. They were shortly joined by aircrews of the Royal Australian Air Force, the Royal New Zealand Air Force, the Royal Canadian Air Force and, when eventually President Roosevelt joined the Allies, he allocated the 492nd Bombardment Group of the United States Air Force.

Charles joined a very cosmopolitan group of over 2,000 personnel at Tempsford airfield, including Norwegians, French, Poles, Czechoslovakians and South Africans. In order to manage the growing demand from the resistance groups, a second Special Duties Squadron was formed. 161 took responsibility for landing and picking up missions leaving 138 the job of parachuting in agents and supplies.

Charles's value as a specialist aircraft radio engineer was especially appreciated by the Special Duties Squadrons and in April 1942 he was commissioned as a flight lieutenant into the technical, signals and radar branch of the Royal Air Force Volunteer Reserve.

Although not documented, Charles would almost certainly have stayed on base or rented accommodation in nearby Sandy or one of the villages in cycling distance from RAF Tempsford. He would have recognised why some described it as 'the foggiest and boggiest' airfield in the UK and others thought it was disused. Most of the buildings for the technical staff, engineering, administration, canteen, officers' and sergeants' mess and living quarters were brick-built but contained a mixture of steel and asbestos. Some were clad in wood and it was said that they were built to resemble animal sheds.

This was Jasper Maskelyne's work. He was an illusionist, famous for his magic shows in London before the war. Surprisingly, these skills were in great demand during wartime. He was appointed a Major and his 'Magic gang' based at the Royal Engineers' Camouflage Experimental Station adapted his conjuring and illusionist expertise to the battlefield on a large scale. His magic was also put into practice at Tempsford. The construction of the site involved the knocking down of several cottages and farm buildings. Port Mahon Farm was occupied by pilots who were taught the vital skill of recognising the silhouettes of planes. The roof slates of Gibraltar Farm were removed to make it look derelict. Windows had the glass deliberately broken. Sacks were draped across the inside of the windows instead of curtains. Some doors were left hanging from only one hinge. For the same reason much of the black Bedfordshire weather-boarding was removed. The adjacent farm buildings got the same treatment.

Inside Gibraltar Farm it was said that the stairs, ceiling and first floor were removed to create a very large room. The inside walls were built up and reinforced. This was to become the airfield's nerve centre. All the hangars and domestic buildings were camouflaged to blend in with the surrounding farmland and it is said that they were all thatched – to give the impression that they were farm buildings. Visitors reported seeing them mildewed, cobwebbed and covered in mould.

Nissen huts resembled pig sties. Outside Gibraltar Farm the pond was left with the odd few ducks. Rusty old tractors were left outside but moved occasionally in the fields and yards. Large grey and green markings and several metres wide black lines were painted on the concrete runways to give the overflying Luftwaffe pilots the impression that they were patches of grass or the continuation of the hedge. Cattle were deliberately grazed on some of the fields when the runways were not in use so that the land might be thought to be being used for agricultural purposes. It succeeded. It is said that the aerial photographs taken by German air crew who flew over the airfield were interpreted as it being disused.

Another secret establishment in Bedfordshire Charles would very likely have visited was Howbury Hall, an 18th century country house set in a large estate near Renhold, about three miles (4.8km) east of Bedford and five miles (8km) west of Tempsford.

In David Hewson's introduction to the reprinted *Moondrop to Gascony*, an account of Anne-Marie Walter's wartime experiences as an SOE courier who was flown out of RAF Tempsford, he suggests Howbury Hall, named by the SOE as Special Training School 40, was opened in early 1943 following serious mistakes by agents handling the S-Phone and the ground-to-air communications system.

According to Stephen Bunker in his *Spy Capital of Britain*, it was under the command of a Major Tidmarsh who had a team of five officers and thirty-seven personnel of other ranks. Whilst it remains undocumented whether Charles worked there, it seems very likely. A ten-day training courses in using the most up-to-date models of Rebecca, Eureka and the S-phone was provided. Those men and women destined to work with the reception committees in Norway, Poland, Czechoslovakia, Denmark, Holland, Belgium, France, Italy, Greece and Yugoslavia needed first-hand experience of using it before they were flown out from Tempsford.

By December 1944, practically all the Special Duty planes had been fitted with 'Rebecca' and, because of the top secret nature of the work it was being used for, its range and frequencies remained classified until the end of the war. Jim Peake, a navigator with 138 Squadron, described Rebecca in his memoirs as a radio beacon consisting of a black box with a retractable 11 foot (3.3 m) aerial. They were lowered out from the back of the plane and had to be wound back in before landing. Some planes had two bi-pole aerials attached either side of the fuselage. The battery-operated, light-weight Eureka transmitters, able to be strapped to someone's chest, were dropped in carefully padded panniers to the waiting reception committee and hidden in hedges or under straw close to the DZ. The ground operator could preset the intensity of the 'blips' to create a radio beam down which the pilot of the aircraft could fly.

The beauty of the Eureka, Peake said, was that it used very little power and could be used to guide an aircraft to a dropping ground without the use of lights or flares, no matter how dark the night. It was only switched on when the approaching aircraft had its Rebecca switched on. Provided that it was sited in a suitable location, pilots could easily guide the aircraft to within 100 yards (91 m) of the box. They had a range of at least 30 miles (48km) at 2,000 feet so navigators did not need recourse to GEE or map reading. Wing Commander Leonard Ratcliff of 161 Squadron reported in his memoirs that he got a Rebecca signal 38 miles from one of his targets. Thanks to Charles and his fellow boffins, there were claims it could be picked up to 60 miles (96 kms.) away.

When the ground-based radio operator learned that the enemy were in the area, they had to move their Eureka sets elsewhere. Sometimes they or a brave resistance member hid them in bundles of firewood tied to theirs backs or the cross bar of a bicycle and tried to avoid a over-curious guard at a check point.

Some of the early Eureka sets were captured in Holland, Belgium and France and were successfully used to guide RAF Tempsford pilots to German-controlled DZs where the containers were dropped. The gunners on the flak batteries were told not to shoot them down until they were on their way back. Captured agents, under torture, had agreed to play back their radio sets to

London in what became known as the 'Englandspiel'. Many agents were arrested on landing and hundreds of resistance group members were identified, arrested, imprisoned, tortured and executed. Thousands of tons of weapons, ammunition, clothes, food, medical supplies and money fell directly into enemy hands.

Consequently, when the double-cross eventually became known in SOE HQ in mid-1943, instructions went out requesting that subsequent Eureka models had to include a self-destruct detonator to avoid them falling into enemy hands.

Brave French steeplejacks positioned two Eurekas, nick-named 'Boot' and 'Shoe', on the pinnacles of Rheims and Orleans cathedrals. This was a great navigational help, as the pilot did not have to fly close to these heavily defended cities. By the end of 1943, Eureka beacons had been planted in three of the great French forests. To help with Operation Market Garden, the Allied invasion of Holland, sets were placed in the Ardennes, wooded hills in eastern Belgium.

Although they were unmanned, a local reception committee was sent in to pick up any containers that were dropped on these 'targets' should the pilot not have been able to spot the correct recognition letter that had to be flashed in Morse code from a hand-held torch on the ground at the designated DZ.

Peake told of how 138 and 161 Squadron planes were fitted with a 6-inch (15 cm) circular screen with a trace line down the centre. A green pulse line projected either side of this line depending on the location of Rebecca. There was a vertical scale between 0 – 90 miles (0 - 144 km) and a switch converted it to 0 – 9 miles (0 - 14 km). By turning a few degrees to port or starboard, the pilot could easily home in. In fact, he wrote, it made the return flight to Tempsford "a piece of cake" for an "idle or tired out Nav."

Michael Foot, the SOE historian, reported that pocket radios were designed to avoid the shortcomings of the rather bulky

Eureka and S-Phones. While SIS developed the 'paraset', which weighed 1.6 kg, a group of Poles working in a factory at Letchworth, produced transceivers that made other Allied equipment look like museum pieces. They were reluctant to let any be handed over to other sections of SOE. Sets, said to cost £12,000 to manufacture in 1944, were issued to agents going into Germany from which they could communicate with radio operators on overflying planes at pre-determined times. (O'Connor, B. *RAF Tempsford: Bedfordshire's TOP SECRET Airfield during World War Two*, private publication)

Whether Charles revisited his old school during the time he spent in Bedfordshire is unknown. The students would undoubtedly have been enthralled by an account of the work he was involved with but, having signed the Official Secrets Act, he was not at liberty to tell anyone what he was doing.

After regularly accompanying special duties' aircrew to install, test and also to operate S-phone and other equipment over France, Charles was posted in June 1944 to SOE's Force 399 in Italy. His prime task was to equip aircraft of the Balkan Air Force with the S-phone and Eureka, thus enhancing the Allies' communication with Josip Broz (Tito) and his communist partisans in Yugoslavia, to whom the RAF were dropping a variety of equipment and liaison officers. The Balkan Air Force also helped the resistance groups in Albania, Greece and Poland. However, his time in Italy was cut short.

I returned to England, as a result of the injuries in Italy and then operated the same kind of activity in Holland but we used (de Havilland) *Mosquitoes for long range penetrations over Germany and for short ranges used the smallest aircraft, the Auster.*

(http://securityriskmanagement.eu/content1.asp? cID=charlesbovill-en 12th December 2009)

In a tribute to Charles's work with the Euro-American Technical Centre for Security Training, it was claimed that he was a close friend of Major Anthony Deane-Hammond. An Internet search revealed that he was Second-in-Command of the 1st Airborne Divisional Signals, one of the British groups involved in Operation Market Garden. This was the planned invasion of Holland in September 1944 which got stopped at what became known as 'The Bridge too Far' over the Lower Rhine at Arnhem. Charles's technical skills in radio equipment were also needed in land transport. On a page on the Major's wartime exploits on the Pegasusarchive website it states that

> ... they were immediately concerned about the distance from the drop zones to the bridge, as they knew that the limited range of their radio sets would result in a blackout between the two areas until on the second day, when the Division was able to advance on Arnhem. To overcome this problem, Deane-Drummond would have liked to have taken more of the powerful Jeep-mounted Type 19 sets that, at present, only the gunners of the 1st Airlanding Light Regiment used. However to take more of these would require additional gliders, of which there were none, and the planning phase for Market Garden was so short that there was no time to work a way around this problem, so Divisional Signals therefore had to make do with what they had. Deane-Drummond noted after Arnhem that absolutely everyone was so keen to get into battle, after so many previous cancellations, that many such risks were knowingly taken.

> Upon arriving in Arnhem, Deane-Drummond was pleased to discover that their radio sets appeared to be working perfectly, but as the 1st Parachute Brigade moved closer towards Arnhem the clarity of their signals began to deteriorate rapidly. Although the Brigade was only two or three miles away at this stage, the medium-range jeep-mounted Type 22 sets were not able to make contact with

them at all. Major Deane-Drummond ordered one of these sets to be driven forward, half way between Divisional Headquarters and the 1st Parachute Brigade, in the hope that messages could be relayed back and forth, however the signal from this jeep quickly faded away.

On Monday 18th September, to inform them of a new radio frequency for the day, Deane-Drummond left Divisional HQ and set out to where the remains of the 1st Parachute Brigade were continuing their efforts to break through to the Bridge.

(http://www.pegasusarchive.org/arnhem/ deane_drummond.htm 13th December 2009)

When the Allies eventually invaded Germany in Spring 1945, Charles was reported by the Euro-American Technical Centre for Security Training website as being on board a plane over Berlin when he used his radio equipment to pick the conversations of Wehrmacht staff, the German military. Whether it had any significance in the final outcome of the war was not mentioned.

The same website refers to his friendship with Captain Sir Basil Liddel-Hart (1895 – 1970), the *Daily Telegraph*'s military correspondent in 1925-32 and military adviser to *The Times* in 1935-9. During the war he wrote for the *Daily Mail* and afterwards became a writer of military history. Exactly what link there was between him and Charles is not known; it was probably in the field of Military Intelligence.

On the day the war finished, which none of us realised was going to occur. I was sent for by the Commanding Officer of the SOE station and he said, "You are out of the action tomorrow. I have a signal from London to say that they have an arrangement with Marconi's that you will return to them on the day upon which the European War ceases."

I flew home next day and two days later I was back at my desk at Marconi's. It was really too much of an anti-climax after all of the excitement. I could not settle down after all the activity. I felt that things were too slow, much as I liked Marconi's. I was sent to take a Frenchman round the British Industry to show our latest developments and amongst the firms visited, was Decca Navigator which Company had just perfected a brilliant new hyperbolic navigation system. I immediately got on very well with Ted Lewis, the chairman, and with Harvey Schwarz, the technical director. He said to me, "Come and run the Air Development side of the Navigator Company. I do not know what you are earning but I will double it if you can start here in a month."

At 34 you do not turn down such offers and I was doing their experiments in the air 5 weeks later. I had 14 wonderful years under Sir Edward Lewis, working all over Europe, France with experiments with their Air Force, Air France, Alitalia, Danish Airlines, American Airlines. Experiments were carried out in over 100 different types of aircraft. Then everything changed, I met a very beautiful lady (Mrs Pamela Keegan (nee Bryan), and we got married.

(Ibid.)

According to his obituary in the *Daily Telegraph*, Charles enjoyed a fulfilling career with Decca, the London-based gramophone manufacturer, where he was much involved with the creation, development and sales of the company's internationally successful Decca Navigator marine equipment.

During his time with Decca, the prnewswire website, reported that the name

...Decca became a piece of nautical terminology that epitomised security and dependability. At its peak there were chains in all of the principal shipping areas of the world and an estimated 200,000 Decca users in Europe alone. By measuring the differences in signals received from transmitters along many of the world's coastlines, mariners and aviators were able to establish their positions with a

Charles Bovill (1911—2001)

degree of accuracy and consistency previously considered impossible. The advent of GPS navigation satellites eventually made the service superfluous and the General Lighthouse Authority, which had been funding Racal to maintain and operate the Decca chains, finally ended its support on 31st March 2000.

(http://www.prnewswire.co.uk/cgi/news/release?
id=19360 4th February 2010)

For understandable reasons, Charles's involvement with Military Intelligence was not mentioned in his obituary. However, a translation of the Euro-American Technical Centre for Security Training website states that

Following the War, Charles Bovill passes depend on reorganization of DI-6 (Department Intelligence-6), real name of the Foreign Intelligence known as MI-6 or S.I.S. (Special Intelligence Service) to develop a incredible technical work on the adaptation and creation Systems, working with the Intelligence Electronic GCHQ UK or in compliance his deep commitment, starting to internal conferences and teaching experience to the American Electronic Intelligence (NSA) to Agents S.D.E.C.E.(Intelligence Defense) or the German MAD (Military Intelligence), in Interception methodologies.

(http://www.eatcst-itd-inc.com/miembros.htm 4th
February 2010)

In the early 1970s he changed jobs yet again. In his interview with Security Risk Management he admitted that

I had been abroad more than 1,000 times and thought that now I wanted to be at home. I left Decca and got a job in London developing Cable TV systems but, whilst I was still young enough, I must get down

to developing devices and systems. I was attracted to technical security as at the time there was a lot of development to do in this field and I have now been in this work for over 20 years. I have a laboratory in the garden of my home and get great satisfaction from the development work which I do and the ECS and Sweeps which I frequently carry out.

(http://securityriskmanagement.eu/content1.asp? cID=charlesbovill-en 12th December 2009)

In 1972 he joined Allen International as their technical director. Soon the showcases at the company's Westminster premises were displaying sophisticated security equipment which was similar to that developed by SOE's boffins in their workshops at the Thatched Barn, a requisitioned hotel on the A1 Barnet by-pass.

During the war they had manufactured "Giglis", a very flexible surgical saw of interlaced cutting wire, which could be concealed in a cap badge, an ordinary boot or shoelace. They were vital for captured secret agents to help them escape from prison cells which had metal bars across the windows. Some bicycle pumps had torches specially built into the handle end. Compasses were hidden in specially-made fountain pens, shaving brushes, hairbrushes, pipes, golf balls and dominoes. Miniature batteries and miniature cameras were sent. Tiny telescopes, one and a half inches long by half an inch wide (39 x 13 mm), were made to look like cigarette lighters! These were some of the 'Q gadgets' provided by the appropriately called Clothing Department of the Ministry of Supply headed by Charles Fraser-Smith. The 'Q War' is the focus of his book *The Secret War of Charles Fraser-Smith.*

Charles Bovill (1911—2001)

Much of the SOE's lethal scientific research and development took place at Station IX, a former hotel called 'The Frythe' near Welwyn, Hertfordshire. It is now a research centre for pharmaceutical giant SmithKline Beecham. As well as delayed action fuses and incendiaries, the boffins developed a silent pistol for assassination jobs, a tear gas gun designed as a pen and cigarettes that blew up when lit. Particularly fascinating were their anti-personnel explosive devices concealed in cavities inside actual everyday objects or in life-size replicas made of plaster or celluloid. These included exploding rusty nuts and bolts, wooden clogs, Chianti wine bottles, screw-top milk bottles, fountain pens, railway fishplates (joint bars), oilcans, life belts, bicycle pumps, food tins, soap, shaving brushes, books, loaves of bread, lumps of coal, rock, turnips, beetroots, stuffed mice and rats and horse, cow and camel dung! Even lethal toilet paper was made.

Agents' wireless transmitting sets were hidden in hollowed-out logs, granite blocks, concrete rubble, faggots (bundles of wood), artists' paint boxes, portable gramophones, office equipment such as adding machines, record players and even bathroom scales, paint and oil drums, car batteries, furniture such as armchairs, cement sacks, vacuum cleaners, driftwood, workmen's tool boxes, electrical testing meters, massage sets and continental wireless sets. Since wireless operators often hid their sets in lavatory cisterns, a lavatory chain was devised, which acted as an aerial. Miniature communication receivers were hidden in clocks, other household goods as well as in hard-backed German Bibles. Few things were sacred in war.

Charles had clearly learned from these devices as his display included microphones disguised as wrist watches and cufflinks, and microphones and radio transmitters attached surreptitiously to ties, fountain pens and table lighters. As the Chief of SOE's

Charles Bovill (1911—2001)

Technical Branch and later General Service Branch MI6, Charles was known affectionately by the International Bodyguard Association as 'Q'. This was the name Ian Fleming gave the quartermaster of the newfangled technology in the James Bond books. In fact,

> *The business provided Q-type gadgets for James Bond films while also building a reputation in the Middle East and elsewhere for security, espionage and counter-espionage equipment. One of Bovill's most effective designs was a crowd-control device which used a photic drive.*

(www.64-baker-street.org/obituaries/ obit_2001_charles_bovill.html 4th February 2009)

With the bomb attacks by the IRA (Irish Republican Army) in London and Birmingham and large anti-government demonstrations during the 1970s and 80s, Charles's equipment was used by the British Police Force. Manchester City Council's Police Monitoring Unit reported that his photic drive was a 10-30 Hz strobe light which produced seizures, giddiness, nausea, and fainting. Adding sound pulses in the 4.0 - 7.5 Hz range increased its effectiveness and it was used in the 'Valkyrie', advertised in the British Defence Equipment Catalogue until 1983 as a "frequency" weapon. In Kim Besley's *Electropollution*, he described the squawk box or sound curdler as using two loudspeakers of 350 watt output to emit two slightly different frequencies which combine in the ear to produce a shrill shrieking noise.

After trying out the device on his wife, Pamela, in his laboratory at West Byfleet, Charles marketed his invention in America, where prison authorities were impressed by its ability to control disruptive inmates and riots. This was despite the U.S. National Science Foundation report which stated that it had a "*severe risk of permanent impairment of hearing.*"

On October 1st, 1973, the staff at Allen International were monitoring one of the firm's spy camera products when they observed a suspicious-looking figure lurking at the entrance. When they confronted the man, he threw a bomb inside the doorway and ran away. The device did not explode but was found to contain five pounds (2.2 kg) of gelignite. Police reports hinted that it had been an IRA attack.

In Klas Nilsson's introduction to the interview he had with Charles, he mentioned that, amongst other things, he had invented the 'Larsen' and the 'Broom'. A clue as to what this equipment was for was the comment that, "*His inventions make the job a lot easier for the professionals within the Electronic Counter Surveillance business.*" An Internet search found Larsen and Broom mentioned in Baron James Shortt of Castleshort's instructional advice to the International Bodyguard Association.

> *The next phase of electronic search is location. This is first done with a piece of equipment called a Larsen which relies on acoustic feedback. Acoustic feedback is what occurs when you take a transmitting microphone too close to a speaker and it starts to howl. However, if the transmitter is not functioning at the time, a Larsen will not detect it. This may be because the device has been remotely switched off (a favourite with the FBI) or because the opposition has bought cheap Chinese batteries and they have drained down (favourite with … well, let's just say they're British!)*

> *If the transmitter isn't transmitting, you need a device called the Broom or Non Linear Junction Detector (NLJD). The Broom was developed by the IBA's ECS instructor Charles Bovill. It detects electronic components whether or not they are transmitting at*

the time. The drawback is that it will also detect TV sets, electronic alarm clocks, microwave ovens and anything else that contains electronic components. The Broom must be used in conjunction with the Larsen. Both these items can be used against telephone devices.

(http://www.iba-deutschland.de/files/iba-baron-castleshorts-instructional-notes.pdf 18th December 2009)

To have left Bedford School at fourteen, gone on to university and become so knowledgeable about ground-to-air radio equipment that he was sent to work with the top secret Special Duties Squadrons during the Second World War is no mean achievement. To have been recognised by military intelligence as a man who could be relied upon to help with specialised electronic equipment and then be headhunted to work around the world with various defence agencies indicates a particularly talented man. To have been compared with 'Q', the character in the James Bond books and have been involved in international electronic counter surveillance technology means that Charles Bovill deserves to be a role model for many a Bedford schoolboy.

This 'Old Bedfordian' continued to experiment and invent in his home laboratory in West Byfleet until shortly before his death in 2001. On his letterhead he stated that he was a Chartered Engineer, a member of the Institute of Electrical Engineers, Fellow of the Institute of Electronic and Radio Engineers and a Member of the Royal Aeronautical Society.

Bibliography

Bunker, S. (2007), Spy Capital of Britain, Bedford Chronicles

Burton, C. Air Power History, *Winter, 2005*

O'Connor, B. (2010), *RAF Tempsford: Churchill''s MOST SECRET Airfield*, Private publication

Smith, C.F., Lesberg, S. & McKnight, G. (1981), *The Secret War of Charles Fraser-Smith*, Michael Joseph, London

The Daily Telegraph,

Walters, A. (2009), *Moondrop to Gascony*, Moho Books, Wiltshire

Websites

http://www.2iemeguerre.com/avions/images/image1468.jpg 18th December 2009

http://www.64-baker-street.org/obituaries/obit_2001_charles_bovill.html 4th February 209

http://www.bandhpast.co.uk/barcombe/b0428build.php11th January 2010

http://www.cvni.net/radio/e2k/e2k035/e2k35cs.html 19th December 2009

http://www.duxfordradiosociety.org/equiphist/reb-eureka/eureka-fig1-598p.jpg 14th December 2009

http://www.duxfordradiosociety.org/equiphist/reb-eureka/eureka-fig4-640p.jpg 14th December 2009

http://www.duxfordradiosociety.org/equiphist/reb-eureka/eureka-fig3-601p.jpg 14th December 2009

http://www.duxfordradiosociety.org/equiphist/reb-eureka/ind96-100-1.jpg 14th December 2009

http://www.duxfordradiosociety.org/restoration/restoredequip/tr3174/tr3174.html

http://www.eatcst-itd-inc.com/miembros.htm 4th February 2010

http://www.gommecourt.co.uk/.../QWR/Bovill%20QWR1.jpg 11th January 2010

http://www.harringtonmuseum.org.uk/138%20Halifax.jpg

Charles Bovill (1911—2001)

18th December 2009
http://www.historyofpa.co.uk/gfx/cw/2lo/girl.jpg 4th
February 2010
http://histru.bournemouth.ac.uk/Oral_History/
Talking_About_Technology/radar_research/assets/
images/p57-img2.gif 14th December 2009
http://www.iba-deutschland.de/files/iba-baron-
castleshorts-instructional-notes.pdf 18th December 2009
http://www.jaapteeuwen.com/.../westland%
20lysander.jpg 18th December 2009
http://www.nwbotanicals.org/oak/newphysics/synthtele/
synthtele.html 18th December 2009
http://www.pathfindergroupuk.com/2005/p_ruvien%
20au%20S-Phone.jpg 14th December 2009
http://www.pegasusarchive.org/arnhem/
deane_drummond.htm 13th December 2009
http://www.r-type.org/static/crystal.htm 10th January
2010
http://www.securitymanager.se/images/Charles_Bovill.jpg
18th December 2009
http://securityriskmanagement.eu/content1.asp?
cID=charlesbovill-en 18th December 2009
http://www.telegraph.co.uk/news/obituaries/1329575/
Charles-Bovill.html
http://www.wired.com/.../2008/09/radio_1921_630px.jpg
10th January 2010

Printed in Great Britain
by Amazon